What People Say About Dr. Shaler...

Dr. Shaler s humor combined with her gentle presence and powerful message make her presentations a "must attend". If you are looking to optimize you company profits and increase effective communication, then make sure you hear Rhoberta. - Ken Foster - CEO, SharedVisionNetwork.com

I really love your book. [Optimize Your Day!] Inspiring information and action planning. It really makes me want to do these things! Thank you so much for this wonderful gift. " Mimi Donaldson, Speaker & Author of 'Negotiating for Dummies

Your ezine [Optimize Life Now] really has helped me a lot over the last 2 years... enough for me to start noticing what a positive effect you've had on me! - Helen, Nova Scotia

What a great perspective! - Jim

I found Rhoberta sparkling, inspiring, soothing, and very practical! Her message was uplifting and delivered with grace and a contagious calm. I highly recommend this expert speaker and masterful practitioner. - D.K. McGuire, Instructional & Quik Reference Designer

What You Pay Attention To EXPANDS

Focus Your Thinking.
Change Your Results.

Rhoberta Shaler, PhD

www.OptimizeLifeNow.com

Copyright 2003 by Rhoberta Shaler, PhD

Although the author, editor and publisher have made every effort to ensure the accuracy and completeness of information contained herein, we assume no responsibility for errors, inaccuracies, omissions, or inconsistencies. We would appreciate receiving feedback on any of the above so they can be addressed in future printings. Please use the contact information below.

Rhoberta Shaler, PhD
WHAT YOU PAY ATTENTION TO EXPANDS.
Focus Your Thinking. Change Your Results.
ISBN: 0-9711689-2-X

Cover design and book layout by Kera McHugh
somethingelse web+graphics, www.time4somethingelse.com

Back Cover Photo of Dr. Shaler Copyright 2000 Nicholas Seiflow, Vancouver, BC Canada

Printed in the United States of America
Published by People Skills Press, San Diego CA

For information, contact:
Optimize Life Now, San Diego CA
Email: info@OptimizeLifeNow.com
Website: www.OptimizeLifeNow.com
Toll Free: 1-877-728-6464

Table of Contents

The more we know
about what we really
want, the better
prepared we are to
recognize favorable chances
and extract good luck.

A. H. Z. Carr

INTRODUCTION

As a young single mother with three children in the days when such a thing was rare, I remember sitting at my kitchen table. On one side, I had a pile of bills and on the other, my checkbook. As I struggled to reduce the pile before the available funds disappeared, a thought struck me. Rather than bemoaning the insufficient funds, I could see it all differently. Instead of my internal conversation being about life being tough and times being hard, money being scarce and electricity being expensive, I could change my attitude. After all, that was one place I was in complete control.

Just then, the phone rang. A friend was inviting me to go along to the movies with her. A lovely offer, but what timing! There I sat with my empty checkbook. Then, it hit me. I had a choice. I could tell her that I would love to go to the movies but life was difficult, I could not afford a babysitter and there were bills to pay. Or, I could tell her that I would love to go but I was choosing to pay the electricity bill this month!

I told her the latter and life has been different ever since. Rather than feeling powerless in the face of endless bills, I could feel powerful in the disbursement of my available funds. My attitude and my view of the situation were entirely within my control.

That was the beginning of my understanding of personal responsibility and choice. From there, I quickly learned that focusing on the power I had rather than on things beyond my control kept me

feeling strong and confident. Once I made that a habit, life changed.

It's been more than thirty years since I first learned that lesson. What I have learned since is that where I choose to look determines the picture I am going to see. It's the old thing about seeing the cup half full or half empty. It's all in the choice. Deciding to see it half-full does not deny that it is also half empty. It simply changes the feelings I experience as a result of the thought. Why not choose the thought that makes me feel better when it is as accurate as the other?

In my view, there is a fine line between positive thinking and denial. Positive thinking is a choice made after accurately assessing an issue and deciding to focus on the most desirable outcome. Denial is unwillingness to admit the issue exists. Big difference!

I've written this book to encourage you to focus on and move towards the outcomes you want rather than the fears or concerns that might keep you from them. You are powerful. You choose where you place your attention. Choose your destination wisely. Keep it clearly in view and you'll get there. I promise because, what you pay attention to expands!

I wish you well.

Rhoberta Shaler, PhD
Optimize Life Now!
San Diego, CA
January, 2003.

There is only one corner of the universe you can be certain of improving, and that's your own self.

Aldous Huxley

The ability to focus attention on important things is a defining characteristic of intelligence.

Robert J. Shiller

KNOW YOUR PURPOSE

Sometimes people forget that meaningful goals—ones they are really willing to accomplish——have to be created in line with their most deeply held values. Ideally you want your top five goals to be completely in line with the top five things you find significant, important and valuable to you.

As a good example of this, I'll tell you about John. He participated in a seminar I gave on "Discovering Your Life's Purpose". John was happy in his work, in fact, he "loved his job", and, yet, life was feeling like a struggle. He felt disjointed, pulled in various directions, and unable to put his finger on the problem.

John seemed clear in his three goals: to expand his sales territory by one state, increase his income by 30%, and to spend one day a week training new staff members. Worthwhile, clear goals, right? As the class explored their deeply held values, John's list had these three at the top: his relationship with his family, his spiritual life and his health.

In order to complete the exercise, John was asked to look at his plans for achieving his goals. They included being out of town frequently. Sometimes he was away a week or so at a time working long days including weekends. Many of his children's activities took place on weekends. When John came home, he was very tired and needed much time to catch up on sleep as well as the work items waiting for him. He missed meeting with his spiritual community on weekends as well.

How were John's goals in line with his values? The way in which John chose to meet his goals was leading him away from what he said he valued. No wonder he was feeling "pulled"! The solution was readily available: John took the weekends out of his travel schedule. Then he was in alignment with his values while still meeting his goals.

When goals and values are not aligned, you experience mixed emotions and a sense of disarray within. Take the time to remember your values and adjust your goals accordingly. Pay most attention to your values.

Remember, what you pay attention to expands.

The secret of getting ahead is getting started. The secret of getting started is breaking your complex overwhelming tasks into small manageable tasks and then starting on the first one.

Mark Twain

By building relations, we create a source of love and personal pride and belonging that makes living in a chaotic world easier.

Susan Lieberman

A SENSE OF BELONGING

Everyone has a need to feel that he or she "belongs". It is a basic human need according to psychologist Abraham Maslow. It is sometimes easy to say that you think you belong—that you have a place in your family or other group—because you know that if you said differently few would accept how you really feel. Deep inside, though, many people feel like observers rather than participants in life!

For many reasons—environment, family, culture, religion, peers—you may have accepted a "less than" feeling about yourself which continuously colors your relationship with yourself and others. There is a great way to lift your spirits and your self-esteem. Here's the secret exercise. Will you promise to do it?

Each morning, when you put your feet over the side of the bed, go directly to the bathroom mirror. Do not clean your teeth, brush your hair or wash your face. Instead, get up close and personal with the mirror. Look yourself directly in your eyes and hold your gaze. Then say, "I love you. I accept you. I approve of you just the way you are." and throw yourself a big kiss! Come on, do it. It is not easy at first to look into your own eyes and say those things to yourself. If you will be persistent, you will be delighted with the results.

OK! You promised! Make that your morning salute to yourself and do it every morning!

Remember, what you pay attention to expands...

Belonging to oneself- the whole essence of life lies in that.

Ivan Sergeevich Turgenev

BUILD ON YOUR BASICS

When you take the time to reflect on what you truly find valuable, important and significant in your life, you can begin to build upon that. It is essential to know what you personally value, not what you have been taught to value, or told to value. It is not a "should", but a personal choice.

It may take some doing to sort this out. Take your time. You are defining the foundation of your life. What a great way to be ready for a fresh look at what's possible for you!

Choose one thing from your list. Let's say that you choose 'loving relationships'. Sit with that thought. Follow it. What is a loving relationship to you? How do you know one when you have one? What are the characteristics? What do you bring to it? What do you want from it? What are you willing to do to have it? What are you unwilling to do? It is this kind of examination of each of your values that allows you to create it fully in your life.

Take that one thing from your list and look for places where you are currently expressing it. It may not be an important value to you if you are not expressing it and keeping it at the forefront of your mind. It may be just a nice idea. If you value it, you seek it out. You create it wherever you are. You think about it, plan for it and look for it.

Remember, what you pay attention to expands.

If we could learn to like ourselves, even a little, maybe our cruelties and angers might melt away.

John Steinbeck

DO YOU NEED PRUNING?

Pruning dead branches helps a tree grow. Do you have any dead branches that need pruning? These could be ideas that are outdated, habits that are non-productive, prejudices that do not serve you. You may have a belief that does not support your growth. Perhaps you accept someone else's idea of what you can and cannot, or should and should not, do. It's time to prune!

When you think about your dreams, what is the first thought that comes to mind—"I can do this!" or "Who am I kidding?" That's the first clue to understanding the need to prune. You may have acquired a negative idea about yourself very early in your life from a teacher or parent who may have only discouraged you once or twice. Of course, you may well have been discouraged more often than that! These can become your "self-prejudices"—your personal fear dragons— and they prevent you from following your dreams.

It seems acceptable, if not rational, to be afraid of new things, doesn't it? Think of your first thoughts about computers! Now it has become socially acceptable to joke about your inability to program a VCR or install new software. That's unwise, you know. That is putting a stamp of approval on your own unwillingness to learn. You are not inept! You can learn to do these things. You know that it is more about your willingness to do so. Let's not encourage a bias against new technology because, really, it is an opportunity to stretch.

Challenging the established ways of thinking always requires courage. In particular, challenging the established ways of thinking about yourself requires courage. Are you ready to think bold, new thoughts about yourself?

Start by pruning, to encourage the new growth. Release useless, outdated thoughts about yourself. Remove habits of thought that limit you. See yourself as able. Keep your eyes on what's possible and STRETCH!

Remember, what you pay attention to expands.

If you don't take charge
of shaping your own
destiny, others will apply
their agenda to you

Eric Allenbaugh

Say nothing good of yourself, you will be distrusted; say nothing bad of yourself, you will be taken at your word.

Joseph Roux

PUT YOURSELF FIRST

If I asked you to describe yourself, what would be the first five things that come to mind? Are they positive things? Are at least three out of five positive? I hope so. If not, though, it is good information. It indicates a need for you to make self-appreciation and self-respect a higher priority.

You've heard the phrase, "Be your own best friend". How would you describe your best friend? It is unlikely that you would have a list of negatives. How do you treat your best friends? With respect, with kindness and understanding, with compassion, right? Treat yourself the same way.

One of my longtime friends recently told me this story. She said that, when she approaches a household task that seems risky, she asks herself, "Would I hire a sixty-seven year old woman to do that for me?" If the answer is "No", then she hires a younger person to do the job. If the answer is "Yes", she proceeds. My dear friend, Helen, is a very wise woman!

If your friend wanted to accomplish something and asked you for support, would you say, "You don't deserve to have it anyway!", "You'll never do it." or "Who are you kidding?"? Probably not, however, you may say things like that to yourself.

What would it take to become your own best friend? What habits of thought would you have to replace? What self-talk would you have to change?

I remind myself of this important phrase often of this:

Never say anything about yourself–out loud or in your head–that you do not want to be true about you.

Would you consider adopting that one for yourself? You'll find that it quickly improves your self-image AND your self-respect.

Remember, what you pay attention to expands.

Have no friends not equal to yourself.

Chinese proverb

If you are clear about
what you want, the world
responds with clarity.

Loretta Staples

THE IMPORTANCE OF INTENTION

Do you know what an important place intention plays in your life? An intention is not only a desire but the determination of a purpose in mind. It is a beginning. Once you intend to change a relationship, it often stays on the top of your mind. If so, the relationship begins to change. How, though, depends upon the intention that you set.

It is common to have conflicting intentions. This often happens with goals. You set a goal to realize part of your vision. You intend to reach the goal. Sub-consciously, you know that when you reach that goal your life will have to be different and you are resistant to that. Your subconscious intention may be to keep things the same. This allows you to talk about moving forward while retaining the familiarity of your life.

Conflicting intentions, then, can throw you into confusion and, often, anguish. It is possible to experience extreme stress and emotional pain when you have conflicting intentions. You can paralyze yourself into inaction.

Intention affects every area of your life. In fact, you begin to change your reality with your intentions. Your dispositions and attitudes are direct reflections of your intentions. You choose your approach to life. Thus, you choose your experience.

Set clear, positive intentions for each area of your life. Examine each intention to uncover subconscious resistances to achieving your desire—and remove them! Focus daily on your conscious intentions and demonstrate that focus by clear, right action in the direction of your vision.

Without action, intention is just cheap conversation.

Remember, what you pay attention to expands.

T he greatest definition
of success is the
progressive
realization of a worthy goal.

Earl Nightingale

A strong positive mental attitude will create more miracles than any wonder drug.

Patricia Neal

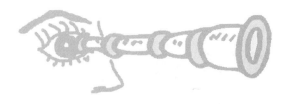

ALWAYS EXPECT THE BEST

Are you expecting things to go well? I hope so. With that focus, you can make each day happier and more productive. It directs your energy towards your goals.

Worrying is an unproductive habit. Has a teenager ever been kept safely on the road by a parent pacing the floor? No, of course not. What is the purpose of worrying? Perhaps it makes the worrier think they are demonstrating concern and responsibility. In truth, it saps energy and attention away from the positive. If you are that parent pacing the floor, visualize the driver coming home safely, hold that thought a few minutes, then do things you enjoy... or sleep well!

Statistics tell us that:

  40% of worries are about events which will never happen
  30% of worries are about events which already happened
  22% of worries are about trivial events
  4% of worries are about events we cannot change
  4% of worries are about real events on which we can act

Clearly, taking action is the only worthwhile thing to do!

If you are worrying about anything, take the time to write down the result you want in rich, evocative, clear language. Include as much detail as you can. Read it over several times, and let go of the concern.

Write down everything you can do to achieve the result you want. Take consistent, positive action to bring it about. This is a good use of your time and energy.

Remember, what you pay attention to expands.

This art of resting the mind and the power of dismissing from it all care and worry is probably one of the secrets of energy in our great men.

Captain J.A. Hadfield

Be gentle with yourself, learn to love yourself, to forgive yourself, for only as we have the right attitude toward our-selves can we have the right attitude toward others.

Wilfred Peterson

IN YOUR QUIET TIME

When you take your quiet time each day—and I hope you do set aside those minutes for yourself—what do you think about? Do you focus on the things that are going well? Do you think about the things that are not going well, and decide on ways to create better results the next time? Do you pay attention to the best next step for you? Those three approaches create benefit. Some folks have a tendency to spend those precious minutes "beating themselves up", or berating them-selves for not being "good enough". Whichever approach you take, remember that you are imprinting your future on your mind. What do you want to create?

You always have choices. You choose your perceptions, your perspective, your reactions, your actions, your words. No one can make you think, say, feel or do anything. Eleanor Roosevelt said, "No one can make you feel inferior without your consent. I believe she was right. How about you?

What happens to you when someone gives you negative feedback? Do you absorb it like a sponge and give it more attention than it deserves? Sure, it depends on who says it and how important the issue is, however, some folks live life just waiting for the negatives. Why? Because it reinforces their belief in their low self-esteem.

Getting things into perspective is not always easy. It takes awareness and willingness. When someone seems to indicate that you are "less than" they think you could be, notice how much value you give to it. Is it in proportion to the

importance of that person in your life, or, is it in proportion to your low opinion of yourself? Is it an opportunity to be discerning, or an opportunity to be self-deprecating? You choose.

Do not let others determine your emotional well-being.

Remember, what you pay attention to expands.

What concerns me is not the way things are, but rather the way people think things are.

Epictetus

To have that sense of one's intrinsic worth which constitutes self-respect is potentially to have everything...

Joan Didion

SEE YOURSELF IN THE BEST LIGHT

Self-image and self-concept are the keys to success! How you view yourself and your role are the basis for everything you do in the world. Add in self-esteem, your level of confidence and satisfaction in yourself, and you have the triple crown! Your self-image sets the boundaries for your level of accomplishment. It defines what you can and cannot do, what you will and will not do, every day.

A positive, realistic self-image is the foundation. Your brain and nervous system operate purposefully to accomplish your goals. There are many ways to enhance this process. Improving your self—image is first! You have a mental "blueprint" of yourself. It is built up from your own beliefs about yourself, many of which have been unconsciously formed from your past experiences—your successes and failures, your triumphs and tribulations—and from the way other peoples have reacted to you, especially in your formative years.

Most of your actions, feelings, and, even your abilities, will be consistent with your self-image. You will act like the person you see yourself as being. Your self-image is the foundation upon which you base your personality, your behavior and your circumstances. Because of this your experiences seem to verify, and thereby strengthen, your self-image and a vicious, or a beneficial, cycle is in motion.

Your self-image can be changed. Your sub-conscious mind is goal-striving in nature. It serves you by making every effort to fulfill your self-image—the way you see yourself and your roles in the world. You are in charge!

Take a few moments to reflect upon your true, current self-image. If it is a little tarnished in some places, decide to view yourself in a more positive, successful light.

Remember, what you pay attention to expands.

Nothing is harder
than to accept
oneself.

Max Frisch

Find the seed at the
bottom of your heart and
bring forth a flower.

Shigenori Kameoka

YOU ARE WHAT YOU THINK YOU ARE

You are what you think you are. And, what you think you are is what you will project to the world. Have you ever noticed that some folks get the "Hey, you" treatment while others get the "Yes, Ma'am" respect. Why is this?

Some folks simply project confidence, poise and assurance while others do not. It is often the case that those who present themselves well are also the most successful.

What is the explanation for this? One word makes the difference: thinking. Thoughts are things and thinking does make things so. You may remember Shakespeare's words" "There is nothing either good or bad, but thinking makes it so." The same is true about how you think of yourself.

You will usually receive the kind of treatment that you think you deserve, even if you do not like it. On the other hand, you are responsible for teaching others how to treat you. If you think you are not good enough, you will project this and allow others to treat you in disrespectful ways. You may resent it. It may make you angry, however, you allow it because you may think you deserve it at some level.

Why not do this differently? Step out with your best self in mind. Know that you are important. If you were not here, there would be an empty space. Take your place. Take up your space and know that you deserve love, respect, attention and acceptance just because you

breathe. Of course, if you persist in doing things that teach others that this is not so, you cannot be surprised if they have a different perception of you, can you? How you think determines how you act. How you act in turn determines how others react to you. It is a simple formula. Look where it starts, though. It starts with how you think. To gain the respect of others, you must first think you deserve respect. The more respect you have for yourself, the more respect others will have for you.

Self-respect is demonstrated by everything you do. Dress well. Your appearance broadcasts how you feel about yourself. Lift your spirits by taking time to look good. No matter how many casual Fridays the work world allows, be sure that you dress in a way that keeps your mind and attitude "thinking sharp". Why do you think the armed services pay so much attention to the details of dressing? Stay sharp.

Your appearance talks to you and it talks to others. You know the line: You never get a second chance to make a first impression. First impressions last far longer than it takes to make one! Start your day with a good impression of yourself. You are what you think you are. What are you projecting?

Remember, what you pay attention to expands....

I think I am one of those who can manage not to take on a completely different appearance under their own glance.

Jean Rostand

Every day begins with an act of courage and hope: getting out of bed.

Mason Cooley

SMALL ACTS OF COURAGE

A successful life requires acts of courage. Fear is a great inhibitor of progress. You must have courage to guarantee success. Courage is acting with resistance to fear or by mastering fear. It is not the absence of fear. Another way to express this is summed up in Susan Jeffers work, "Feel the Fear and Do It Anyway!"

Sir Winston Churchill proclaimed that,

"Courage is the first of human qualities because it is the quality that guarantees all others.

Without courage, you might not get out of bed in the morning! Courage demonstrates your willingness to participate fully in life. Courage is the quality that enables you to face the challenges of the day and overcome obstacles to achievement. Courage makes it possible for you to speak up when it would be easier to remain silent, to work when you don't particularly feel up to it. Courage keeps you moving forward, tackling challenges and tasks until they are solved and completed.

You are not born with courage. It is a dynamic trait, developed through action, that grows with use. Courage develops as you confront the people, situations and tasks which you fear. As you do this, you discover that you have all the talents and abilities required to carry you through to achieving your goals. When you act with courage,

you also attract others to you and your work. Courage demonstrates your belief in yourself!

Fear of the unknown is probably one of the major enemies of courage. Knowing this helps you to overcome it. Exercise your power of choice and have an attitude of positive expectancy. Be a leader in your own life.

Goal-setting helps to eliminate fear. When you take the time to examine any obstacles that stand between you and the achievement of your goals, you are looking fear in the face. You have turned the "unknown" into the "known". Then you can determine specific solutions to overcome each obstacle.

Courage reflects your growing desire and willingness to be who and how you most want to be, to have the kind of life you most want, and to be successful in the ways that are most important to you. Goal-setting promotes courage. Achieving your goals is the result of your courage.

Developing courage gives you the ability to turn plans into action, dreams into goals, and success into reality. Be courageous!

Remember, what you pay attention to expands.

Face the fearful with no fear, and its fearfulness disappears.

Chinese proverb....

Each morning the day lies like a fresh shirt on our bed. The happiness of the next twenty-four hours depends on our ability, on waking, to pick it up.

Walter Benjamin

GREET THE DAY

What were your first few thoughts as you opened your eyes this morning? What feelings did they evoke? What impetus did they give to your day?

When you get up each morning, do you have something to look forward to? You are in charge of your life. You have the option to create that "something" each day. You may even have already exercised that option and created days filled with things about which you are passionate and in which you are fully engaged. Did you?

For many folks, the next thought they would be having right this minute is "Yes, but.... We are so good at thinking about barriers and obstacles that can serve as reasons and excuses. It is important to ask yourself what the real truth about matters is—and to be completely honest with yourself—no matter what!

Oh, does that sound harsh to you? It might if you are new to the idea of 100% personal accountability, I suppose. I'm sure you are well-aware that there really is no one to blame in this world for the way you choose to live from moment to moment. Inconvenient, but true!

No matter where you are in this world, you always have the option to choose your perception and response each moment. It does not matter what your past has held. You are the only one holding onto it!

Give yourself something special to look forward to each day. Make a commitment to do that!

You will enjoy the difference it makes in your life. It does not have to be big...it just has to "be"!

Remember, what you pay attention to expands.

Think in the morning. Act in the noon. Eat in the evening. Sleep in the night.

William Blake

In the long run, we get no more than we have been willing to risk giving.

Sheldon Kopp

SIMPLE CONCEPTS

Some of the simplest concepts in life seem to be the most difficult to put into practice. A concept is "*something conceived in the mind*" and often, even the most beneficial ones are left there.

You may talk about these ideas and share them with others, discuss their merits and indicate your approval. But, what action do you take? Consider the concept of regular exercise or eating well, managing stress or stopping smoking. Conversations abound with stated intentions, expected benefits and, even, starting dates. But, what happens?

Doing something—actually taking action—on a concept that you consider to be life-enhancing is a definite statement of your self-worth! Say, "I love myself, therefore, I choose to look after my body. I am important so I'll make time for me. When you give, you receive. An interesting paradox...and a simple concept!

Do you know that this simple Universal Law works in every area of your life? Do you want more love in your life? Focus on giving your love freely. Do you want more attention, respect or acceptance? More trust? Give it! Be it!

Change your focus from getting to giving and you will find much more joy in your daily living. There is no scarcity. You live in a world of infinite supply. So, give. Give freely. Give willingly.

Remember, what you pay attention to expands.

There are no short cuts to any place worth going.

Unknown

HANG IN THERE

Do you keep on keeping on when you really want something? Many times, folks give up too soon. In fact, there are some who say that most folks give up far too readily. It seems to me that the problem is not only in the giving up but in the lack of real desire in the first place.

Do you know the difference in feeling between something you really, really want, and something that would be nice to have? The first is passion; the second is recognition. The first stirs you to action; the second, comfortable inaction. What do you really, really want to achieve, have, be, experience, feel? How important is it to you?

All achievement has its beginnings in an idea. It is like a seed. You find it, plant it, nurture and nourish it. It grows, matures and blooms. Finding the seed, the idea, is only the beginning. Nothing will bloom that stays in the seed packet, will it? Plant your ideas in the fertile ground of your mind. This is intention. Nurture and nourish them with daily attention. Visualize and affirm what they will become. Stay constant.

Keep them in mind even when you are away from them. Pay special attention in "bad weather". Appreciate and enjoy them when they flower. Remain grateful. Plant again.

Remember, what you pay attention to expands.

What others say of me matters little: what I myself say and do matters much.

Elbert Hubbard

WHAT DO YOU SAY WHEN YOU TALK TO YOURSELF?

What do you say when you talk to yourself? Are you complimentary? Are you encouraging? I believe it is important to say only things about yourself, and to yourself, that you want to be true. Why? Because you are listening!

You learn in so many ways. You can learn to be a goal-setter, to be more creative, to relate to others better and to think positively. You can learn the secrets of success. You may have done all these things. They are inspirational and may get you going for a while. Where, though, is the staying power of those messages?

The human brain is an incredibly powerful personal computer, your control center. It is capable of doing anything reasonable that you'd like it to do, but, you have to know how to program it. If you do that in just the right way, giving it careful directions, it will do the right thing. It will work for you in the right way.

It is estimated that an average person growing up in a reasonably positive home was told "No!" or what they could NOT do, more than 148,000 times! That is considerable negative programming by any standards. Even half that many times would be too many!

"Leading behavioral researchers have told us that as much as seventy-seven percent of everything we think is negative, counterproductive and works against us. At the same time, medical researchers have said that as much as seventy-five percent of all illnesses are self-induced. It's no wonder. What if the researchers are correct? That means that as much as seventy-five percent or more of our programming is the wrong kind."* And most of us took it to heart!

When you hear the same words and thoughts repeatedly, it etches itself in your mind and you take it to heart. Repetition is a convincing argument. Unless we erase or replace that negative programming, it will stay with us permanently. It will affect and direct our thoughts and actions. Change your programming now. You can!

Remember, what you pay attention to expands.

* This statement came from Shad Helmstetter in *What To Say When You Talk To Yourself,* MJF Books, 1986. I highly recommend this book.

You can succeed if others do not believe in you. But you cannot succeed if you do not believe in yourself.

Dr. Sidney Newton Bremer

Do a little more each day than you think you possibly can.

Lowell Thomas

PERSISTENCE PAYS

Are you persistent? Do you know how important that can be to your personal and professional success?

Folks who have cultivated the habit of persistence almost seem to enjoy some insurance against failure. No matter how many setbacks they experience, they continue and they usually get where they planned to go. Sometimes it seems that these setbacks are simply tests to see how committed they are to their goals. If something is very important to you, and you persist, you may even exceed your goals. Persistence pays.

Very successful people are often the ones who viewed setbacks, defeats or failures as urges to greater effort. When you read biographies of these folks, they seldom had easy roads to their goals and dreams. They often exhausted and exasperated themselves and the folks around them on their journeys. They may have also exhausted their resources, yet, they picked themselves up, faced in the direction of their vision, and walked on. Do you?

Think of the actors on Broadway and in Hollywood. Those "overnight sensations" usually took fifteen or so years of hard work and dedication, didn't they? Think of Henry Ford who went bankrupt twice before he finally started the Ford Motor Company. Think of Michael Jordan who began his illustrious career by being cut from his high school basketball team. Even Dr. Seuss had his manuscripts rejected...as well as Albert Einstein. What great company to find yourself in!

If things don't seem to be coming your way, go after them. Persist and pursue them anyway. You'll be glad that you did!

Remember, what you pay attention to expands.

People who are resting on their laurels are wearing them on the wrong end.

Malcolm Kushner

Life is a process of becoming, a combination of states we have to go through. Where people fail is that they wish to elect a state and remain in it. This is a kind of death.

Anais Nin

GET OUT OF THE PAST

How much time do you spend in thinking about events, situations and circumstances that have already passed? How much energy do you give to these things? Are there unresolved relationships that need your attention? Are there unfinished tasks that bother you each time you think of them? All these things need taking care of....and, as soon as possible.

The brain operates on a binary system. It can only pay attention to one thing at a time. True, it can move from one idea, perception, thought to another very rapidly, yet, it can only pay attention to one thing at a time. You choose what it pays attention to. True, too, it often does not seem that way. Your mind races. Thoughts come so quickly they are fleeting. You do choose what the mind dwells on, though.

Do you choose to stop on the good times or the distressing events most often? Do you focus on when you felt strongest or weakest? Do you think about what you have done well or when you have made mistakes? If you think about a mistake, do you think about it to create a plan of action so that it will not recur, or, do you beat yourself up about it? Two very different ways to use the past!

Many times in seminars I will ask participants to state what they most want in life. Most folks are quick to say what they do not want, what they never want to happen again. It seems, for them, that the past has

been a great teacher of what to avoid! What DO you want to move towards? Focus on IT!

Have you ever made a treasure map, a visual affirmation of what you want? It's fun as well as being a great tool for focus and inspiration.

Just take a large piece of poster board, cut out pictures and words that represent all the things you want to bring into your life—relationships, vacations, money, jobs, attributes, traits, reunions—and make a collage. You can be as artistic as you like. When you have everything on the page that you wish to attract, write an affirmation for each and paste it onto the treasure map. Place this map in a prominent location so you will see and read it every day. This is a powerful technique for creative focus and visualization.

Remember, what you pay attention to expands.

Though no one can go back and make a brand new start, anyone can start from now and make a brand new ending.

Carl Bard

D on't be afraid your life will end; be afraid that it will never begin.

Grace Hansen

YOU HAVE THE OPPORTUNITY OF A LIFE TIME

You have the opportunity of a lifetime. That sounds like marketing hype because you have heard it so often, doesn't it? Think about it this way: you have the opportunity to live one lifetime. Does that make a difference? How are you using your opportunity?

Are you doing the things you want to be doing in the ways that you want to be doing them? If not, why not? What are you viewing as obstacles to having the life you want? Are the obstacles you perceive real or just convenient? So often it is comfortable to complain about them. Sometimes folks think that acknowledging the obstacle in this way relieves them of the requirement to overcome them. Could that be you?

What is the first thing that comes to mind when you hear the question, "What do you REALLY want?" Do you know? Are you clear? That's the beginning. When you can very clearly state what you do want, then, you are on your way!

The next step is to be able to picture having what you want.

Can you feel, hear and see yourself living the lifestyle you most want? It's important to be able to do this. Your mind works in pictures, so make yours a good one.

Spend some time each day picturing your ideal life in great detail...even just five or ten minutes will do. Be prepared for some changes in your life when you make this a habit because they will come.

Remember, what you pay attention to expands.

When you come to the edge of all you know, and are about to step off into the darkness of the unknown, faith is knowing one of two things will happen: There will be something solid to stand on, or you will be taught how to fly.

Barbara J. Winter

When we are
motivated by
goals that have
deep meaning, by dreams
that need completion, by
pure love that needs
expressing, then we truly
live life.

Greg Anderson

WOULD YOU RATHER BE WEALTHY?

Would you rather be wealthy or poverty-stricken? Not a difficult question to answer, is it? How do you think your thoughts impact on your financial state?

Just as the earth contains in its depths great riches—oil, diamonds, gold, uranium, silver, gas and countless other things—you also have the real riches of life deep within you. Your innate intelligence and your willingness to use your mind are precious. Begin mining within!

There is a great story about a poor miner in Scotland who was often unable to even provide shoes for his children. His young son came to him and told him that he wanted to be a surgeon. His father asked him why he wanted that career and he said that a friend at school had had cataracts. An eye surgeon had operated on his friend and now he could see perfectly. The young boy said that he wanted to be able to help people in that same way.

The father told his son that he had saved $8,000 for his education but would prefer that he worked his way through medical school and then use that money to set himself up in a medical practice in a fine neighborhood. The boy did so. He worked nights and weekends and finally graduated. He wanted to live up to his promise to his father and not touch the money in the bank until he graduated.

When he graduated, his father told him that there really was no money in the bank. The new surgeon was completely at a loss for words for a few minutes. Then both he and his father burst out laughing. The son realized that his father had really engendered the feeling of wealth in his son and it had given him the courage, faith and confidence to believe in his ability to earn his way through medical school.

The secret of success, accomplishment, achievement and fulfillment of your goals lies in the discovery of the amazing power of your thoughts and feelings. You must come to a clear-cut decision that you intend to be successful. Impress your subconscious with love, confidence, right action, abundance, security and good humor and it will always be there for you to "mine"! What you keep in mind, you will create.

Remember, what you pay attention to expands.

It is our attitude at the beginning of a difficult undertaking which, more than anything else, will determine the successful outcome.

William James

The definition for peak productivity: the use of your time, energy, intelligence, resources and opportunities in a manner calculated to move you measurably closer to meaningful goals.

Dan Kennedy

NEW BEGINNINGS

Do you know what you like? Do you know what is right for you? Brian Tracy says that it is important to know what is right for yourself before you think of what is possible. Do you know what brings you joy? If you do know, how often do these things show up in your life? Do you plan for them?

It is interesting—and powerful—to focus your attention on what you want in life, experiences you want to repeat, attributes you wish to develop, goals you long to reach and, fulfilling ways to spend your time and energy. When you keep your mind, time and energy on these things, there is little time for anything else—and the "anything else" fades away!

When you set your goals, do so very carefully. Make a balanced plan with goals in each area of your life to move your physical, social, educational, financial, mental, emotional and spiritual self forward. Once you have decided on the priorities, assign a daily, weekly, monthly or annual amount of time for each that will satisfy you. This is important. There is no right answer.

What will cause you to feel good about yourself when you do it? It can be different for different people. Some folks want to run a marathon and that is what they mean when they are planning to improve their exercise program. That will take more time than for a person who wants to increase their time doing weight-bearing exercise to prevent osteoporosis. Know what your goal is and why. That will help you assign the appropriate amount of time to each priority.

Make sure that your goals are "do-able". Build in success this way. Make them very specific, measurable and time-bounded. Your mind can capture a goal that says, "I will lose ten pounds by March 1 by eliminating ice-cream from my diet and walking three miles three times a week", whereas it has difficulty understanding "I am eating less and exercising more." Be specific.

Often, there are many things undone in our lives. Things we wish we had done, things we know are always sitting at the back of our minds draining our energy. These are 'energy leaks'. You know the "(Expletive) I still haven't _____ yet!" that hits you while you're waiting for a red light to change. It's a 'leak'!

Here is a process that I find amazingly effective. Complete the PERSONAL INTEGRITY CHECKLIST to start your year with no energy 'leaks'. Clearing away your energy leaks is a good preparation for being successful with your new plan.

Remember, what you pay attention to expands.

Get the Personal Integrity Checklist, free, from my website: www.OptimizeLifeNow.com

The person who makes a success of living is the one who sees his goal steadily and aims for it unswervingly. That is dedication.

Cecil B. DeMille

How I Spend My 168 Hours...

family _ _ _ _ _
career _ _ _ _ _
grooming _ _ _
sleep _ _ _ _ _
exercise _ _ _ _
driving _ _ _ _ _
household _ _ _
community _ _
recreation _ _ _
alone _ _ _ _ _

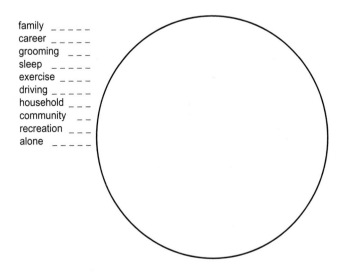

YOUR 168 HOURS

In every week you have 168 hours to use as you wish. Do you really know how you spend them? A general idea of what you do with your time is not nearly as instructional as a clear understanding. Here is an exercise to help you clarify.

Take a letter-size piece of paper and draw a large circle on it. To the right of the circle, write these words in a vertical list: family, career, grooming, sleep, exercise, driving, community, household, recreation, time alone...add any that are important to you. Now, beside each item, put the number of hours in an average week that you spend on it. When you are done, change those numbers into a percentage of your 168 hours/week. Now, to really make an impact, make a pie graph in the circle of the ways you spend your time.

If, by any chance, you simply read the above paragraph without doing the exercise, and are now reading this, STOP! Nothing changes until you do. If you do not know how you spend your time, you will not receive the full benefit of the ideas in this article. It is not enough to be saying to yourself, "I know that I need more time for _____. If that is so this exercise will help you find it. Please, won't you go back and make the chart now? (This may be one of the ways you short-change yourself in your daily life. You may not give yourself time to do the good and beneficial things that you know would improve your life. Is that a pattern for you?)

Once you have your pie divided, ask yourself if the graph well represents the importance of each item to you at this time in your life.

You may have to have quite a conversation with yourself to determine this. Remember, there are not any right answers...just right answers for you!

If you find that your graph fits your priorities, you will be experiencing contentment. If not, you may want to make some adjustments.

Remember, what you pay attention to expands.

P

eople find life entirely
too time-consuming.

Stanislaw Lec

To freely bloom - that is my definition of success.

Gerry Spence

WHAT YOU PAY
ATTENTION TO EXPANDS

OK, so, what you pay attention to, expands. As with most things, what you pay attention to is a choice. There is no unwritten law that commands you to wallow in the negative; to call up your friends and regale them with the "isn't-it awful" and "they-done-me-wrongs". It is entirely your choice.

The Buddhist monk, Thich Nhat Hanh, who lives in France and writes uplifting books about peace and compassion says:

> "People deal too much with the negative and what is wrong... Why not try and see positive things, to just touch those things and make them bloom?"

Are you blooming or withering?

I am not advocating living in a state of denial, pretending that nothing is wrong and that things never go in directions you don't like. That kind of "positive thinking" is unhealthy. Just be mindful of where, how, and for what purpose, you use your energy.

You choose what you think and talk about. Of course, there are unpleasant things in life that sometimes require your attention. Create a positive solution for yourself and move towards it directly. Give up complaining. You'll be happier and so will those around you.

For today, focus on what you want to bring into your life and use your energy accordingly? Notice what you pay attention to and gently refocus on the positive.

Bloom where you are planted!

Remember, what you pay attention to expands.

Accentuate the Positive; Eliminate the Negative; Latch on to the Affirmative; Don't mess with Mr. In-Between.

Johnny Mercer

About the Author...

Rhoberta Shaler, PhD, speaks, coaches & conducts seminars for entrepreneurs & professionals who want the motivation, strategies and inspiration to achieve, to lead and to live richly. She has spent over 30 years teaching, encouraging and inspiring thousands of people to look at their personal and corporate lives from a new perspective. Rhoberta challenges them to create integrity between their plans and their daily practices, their beliefs and their behaviors. Her commitment to finding passion in life and pursuing it is contagious.

A Canadian, she currently lives in San Diego, CA, with her husband, Keith Couch. Rhoberta loves to meet new people, go to the theater, read, walk, knit, travel and spend time with her family, friends and colleagues. She is a member of the National Association of Female Executives and the National Speakers Association.

Presentation Information

Dr. Shaler speaks to thousands of people each year giving them and their organizations 'The OK's to SUCCEED!" --the Optimization Keys to lift their sights and elevate results from acceptable to EXCEPTIONAL.

Her Living Richly" Accelerated Achievement Program and Living Richly" Weekends offer intensive personal development for people ready to take their lives to the next levels. You can sponsor a one-day or two-evening, Living Richly" Seminar in your area. Offer this as a value-added bonus to your members, clients or staff. See the website for details. www.OptimizeLifeNow.com/LR

Rhoberta's complete press kit is available online. You'll find detailed descriptions of her keynotes and programs, testimonials, client list, biography and photos for booking and media use. Call toll-free, 877.728.6464, to book Dr. Shaler to bring your people the motivation and strategies to achieve, to lead and to live richly now.

Other Products From Dr. Shaler

All products can be ordered securely online through Dr. Shaler's website. We accept all major credit cards, online checks, mail and fax orders.

Audio Tapes:

Living Richly" Eight Essentials for Having the Life You Want - An 8-cassette or 2-CD Seminar

Living Richly" Home Study Program - An 8-cassette or 2-CD self-directed program with companion workbook

You Are the Mastermind of Your Masterpiece - Make Your Life a Work of Art. Examine your current path and create the life you want.

Be Positively Selfish/Be A Real Goal Getter - Strategies to bridge the gap between goals and measurable results. Get you what you want in life.

Attitudes Heal: Change your way of thinking... change your health.

Cancer Is A Challenge: Strategies for managing through a diagnosis and living beyond it.
Fighting Fires Without Burning Bridges Communication and Conflict Management.

Stories, Stars & Sticky Rice: Creating Success on Your Own Terms

Don't Tell Me to Calm Down! Managing Anger -Yours & Theirs

Get Your Ducks in a Row! Encouraging Self-Esteem, Self-Awareness & Self-Confidence in Young Children

Books:
The Handbook to Living Richly" Eight Essentials to Creating the Life You Most Want

Optimize Your Day! Practical Wisdom for Optimal Living

What You Pay Attention To Expands. Focus your thinking. Change your results.

Prevent Freefall: Pack Your Own Parachute. Timely tactics for taming tense times (booklet)

Visit
www.OptimizeLifeNow.com
for these and other products.
They make great gifts for
family, friends, colleagues
and clients!